I Don't Bow to Budd

I Don't Bow to Buddhas

Selected Poems of Yuan Mei

Translated from the Chinese and
with an introduction by J. P. Seaton

COPPER CANYON PRESS

Publication of this book is supported by a grant from the National Endowment for the Arts and a grant from the Lannan Foundation. Additional support to Copper Canyon Press has been provided by the Andrew W. Mellon Foundation, the Lila Wallace–Reader's Digest Fund, and the Washington State Arts Commission. Copper Canyon Press is in residence with Centrum at Fort Worden State Park.

Library of Congress Cataloging-in-Publication Data
Yuan, Mei, 1716–1798
I don't bow to Buddhas: selected poems of Yuan Mei/translated
by J.P. Seaton
p. cm.
ISBN 1-55659-120-9 (pbk.)
1. Yuan, Mei, 1716-1798 – Translations into English.   1. Seaton,
Jerome P.   11. Title
PL2735.A5I17 1997   96-51284
895.1'348 – DC21

COPPER CANYON PRESS
PO Box 271, Port Townsend, Washington 98368

For K, J, C, and T
*wife, sons, daughter
and best friends*

Contents

Introduction

WHAT SORT OF A MAN was this Chinese poet Yuan Mei (1716–1798), who would "not bow to Buddhas"?

He was a feminist, a democrat, a gourmet and a "food writer," a sensualist and a family man. As a young man he was a star of the Imperial Civil Service Examination system; in early maturity, an enormously successful official who was not altogether willingly an early retiree from office. In later life he was the author of how-to books on writing in the rigidly formal examination essay style, a collector and editor of tales of the supernatural and of psychic phenomena, and a religious skeptic who was nonetheless profoundly influenced by Ch'an (Zen) Buddhism. Throughout his life he was extraordinarily influential as a poet, literary critic, and poetry teacher, and was patron and friend of writers both Chinese and Manchu. On the side he was a landscape architect who made his own private garden open to the public for festivals and recreation. A self-proclaimed bookworm, and a self-consciously witty commentator on the ways of the world, Yuan Mei was the last great poet of the classical Chinese tradition and perhaps the most popular Chinese poet in the 2,500 years of the tradition. His works, often written in something very close to the colloquial spoken language of his time, appealed both to the classically educated literati and to the literate townspeople of Ch'ing Dynasty China, a burgeoning class of men and women whose taste helped to establish literature in the colloquial as the true cultural flower of the period.

Arthur Waley's fine biography of the poet (deservedly still in print after fifty years, from Stanford University Press) shows a great deal of the complexity of the man, develops his life chronologically, gives excellent historical background, and, in addition, offers a broad and well-translated sample of his poetry. I will leave it to you to test the apparent hyperbole, and the seemingly paradoxical statements in the beginning of this introduction, if you wish, by reading that biography. It's a book worth reading as much for the simple enjoyment of Waley's own wit and elegant prose as for its portrait of the enlightened humanist Yuan Mei.

There is an old Chinese saying, "The Three Ways are One." Western students of Chinese culture often find the saying a fine example of the supposed "inscrutability" of the Chinese. Confucianism is famous for its artificiality and its inflexibility. Taoism is admired for its mystical naturalism and its emphasis on spontaneity. The two are joined, perhaps, only in their rejection of the supernatural, and through that rejection they are both apparently at odds with institutional Buddhism. The reduction of the paradox is made possible, and even *necessary*, in the Chinese worldview by the presence of the overarching influence of the concepts of Yin and Yang. The harmonious balance of action and inaction, creative and nurturing forces, of the pragmatic and the imaginative – embodied in the graphic symbol the T'ai Chi – is the underlying image of *perfection* in nature, in society, and in the individual consciousness within traditional Chinese culture. Yuan Mei the man, and the poet, offers a perfect embodiment of the ideal. His scholarship, his success in the Civil Service Examinations, his effective service to the people while in government office, and even his retirement from office, which can be seen as a protest against the Manchus' authoritarian government: all of these things mark a formal commitment to the highest values of Confucianism. If his poetry, and his literary criticism as well, also identify him as an opponent of the dominant formalistic orthodoxy known as Neo-Confucianism, based on the classical commentaries of Chu Hsi, they also mark him as a strong proponent of its heterodox alternative, the radically democratic Confucian syncretism of the Ming Dynasty activist philosopher Wang Yang-ming. It is obvious that Yuan Mei, in his own individualistic manner, firmly embraced the Yang of Confucianism.

In his retirement it is equally easy to see the poet's embracing of the Yin, in the form of the epicureanism and artistic spontaneity supported by the authority of Lao Tzu and Chuang Tzu, the pillars of philosophical Taoism. The life of attentive ease presented in the poems in this selection might easily be seen as the very embodiment of the Yin of the Taoist Way.

Yuan Mei rejected the debased popular Taoism of his time. He also rejected forms of Buddhist belief and practice that could be seen to parallel the superstitious practices of the popular Taoists. While popular Taoism was largely limited to the lower classes, institutional Buddhism was a fundamental support for the moral repression and puritanism of the Neo-Confucian orthodoxy. Many of Yuan Mei's associates in government were ostensibly Buddhists, and several openly criticized Yuan as a libertine, focusing on his sexual behavior in particular. The fact that such criticism also mentioned his democratic treatment of women and members of the lower classes as symptomatic of fundamental "impiety" makes it clear that it was liberal and not libertine behavior that provided the motivation for his critics.

Yuan Mei was born in 1716, into genteel poverty. His father, a relatively unsuccessful minor official, traveled widely and for the most part lived separately from his family. Yuan was raised by his mother and an aunt. He was a much-loved child and, by his own admission, a spoiled child. He was, by general consensus, a child prodigy. He listened avidly to the stories from Chinese history told to him by his Aunt Shen even as he was beginning the arduous process of mastering the written language. At the age of six he was provided with an excellent teacher, a Mr. Shih Chung, whom he remembered fondly in his later years. He discovered and devoted himself to poetry at an early age, and he also excelled at his classical studies. As with every good son of an official, and as with surprisingly many literate males of all classes in eighteenth-century China (where literacy was high even by modern Western standards), his early years were spent primarily in preparation for the Imperial Civil Service Examinations. In the Ch'ing Dynasty this process began with the rote memorization of the orthodox Neo-Confucian versions of the Classics, the "Four Books" as established by Chu Hsi of the Sung, and led ultimately toward the mastery of a special prose form, the "eight-legged essay," a nasty poison spider of lock-step rigidity to be constructed in response to equally nasty little pedantic questions. The point of view of the Manchu rulers of the Ch'ing was one that promoters of a male Caucasian version of "cultural unity" in our own time might well understand and applaud: the student must accept the structures of conventional knowledge and rigid discipline, to learn, in essence, to *willingly* put his nose to the masters' grindstone until he (or it) had gotten the point. The Examination system had become a tool of authoritarianism, and a very good one, at that.

In 1736, with official patronage and high expectations, the young Yuan Mei, having passed a series of qualifying exams, went off to the capital to take part in a Special Examination. Much to his surprise and dismay, he failed. No more poetry for a few months, we may safely assume, and back he came in 1738, to take a lesser degree. The following year, at the ripe old age of twenty-three, he took and passed the final *chin shih* degree, and, upon passing the ultimate Palace Examination, under the eyes of the Emperor, was rewarded with the most prestigious of prizes, an appointment to the famous Hanlin Academy. There, sequestered in weeks-long shifts "on call" as court poet and document drafter to the Emperor himself, he very quickly showed that his own tastes were well suited to the traditional homosexual habits of the institution. In later life he would maintain this predilection, while apparently developing an increasingly strong interest in the opposite sex. He was to be praised in some quarters, but damned in many, for openly referring to both facets of his erotic life in his poetry.

After his stint in the Hanlin Academy, Yuan held several minor but increasingly important government posts, culminating in 1745 with an appointment as Prefect of Nanking, the beautiful city by the Yangtze River that was the cultural center of eighteenth-century China. At that time his political career met its first real fork in the road: in 1747, he expected an appointment as Governor of Kao-yu, near Yangchou, but the appointment didn't come. The alien Manchus ruled Ch'ing China, and they required that Chinese aspirants to high office have a knowledge of their non-Chinese language. For one reason or another, Yuan Mei had done very poorly on his Manchu language examination. He had cultivated a few very prominent Manchu patrons, but they failed him here. Perhaps they felt he needed a lesson. He'd been popular as an official, so popular indeed that the common people, native Chinese like himself, had praised him in folk verse. At any rate, in the face of official disappointment he made a fateful choice. The ancient Taoist Yang Chu was known to weep at a crossroad, knowing that every choice led to yet another, every crossroad to another crossroad. Yuan Mei may have smiled as he made his choice in 1748, buying land in Nanking: a place formerly owned by a man named Sui, who'd built a garden there. It was overgrown now. He'd fix it up a bit while he waited for what would surely be a triumphal return to office. The poetry he wrote in praise of his new enterprise reveals that he expected such a return.

Time passed and no call came. Eventually, reduced by circumstances to presenting himself for a minor position, he made his way north from Nanking to ancient Ch'ang-an, now a provincial capital, in 1752. His path is strewn with poems that suggest his dismay, even perhaps his disgust. After only three days in office, news of his father's death gave him an excuse to resign the post he'd accepted reluctantly. This last fork in the Way led back to Nanking, where, at the age of thirty-six, he began a career as a private man that was to last nearly fifty years.

When he bought his Nanking garden he changed the character for the first syllable of the name of the garden from the Chinese character *Sui*, used for the family name of the original owner, to another character, also pronounced *sui*, but meaning literally "to follow." This character is a word replete with literary allusions and connotations of doing as one pleases or being free and at ease. The character for "garden" in Chinese is pronounced *yuan*, and is thus homophonous with Yuan Mei's family name. The character is, in fact, constructed of two major elements. The first element encountered is an outer rim or square "box," emblematic of a wall. The other element within the "wall" is structurally the "phonetic" element; it gives the pronunciation of the character as a whole. When it stands alone, it is pronounced *yuan*, and means "a robe." It is also the character that served as Yuan's surname. The wordplay is typically Chinese. How better to say *my* garden, where I will suit myself, and be myself? It is illuminating to note that, true to his egalitarian nature, Yuan actually chose not to surround the physical garden with a wall, and throughout his life made it available to the people of Nanking, very much like a public park. Certainly there was no exclusive wall around the man, either.

After those few short days as an official in old Ch'ang-an, Yuan Mei never again held office. For the traditional Chinese gentleman of talent and ambition (and certainly Yuan Mei possessed both qualities), such a choice was at best an ambiguous one. The ideal Confucian serves the Emperor for the purpose of serving the people. The meaning of his life is in that act. He is an idle fool or a hedonistic rogue if he refuses such service – or is he perhaps a passive critic of his sovereign, a potential rebel? It is always hard to tell. Friends and former colleagues went to their deaths in the literary inquisitions of the eighteenth century. Yuan Mei avoided the political stage, safe behind the metaphorical wall of his retirement. Marking himself as an eccentric in a society where the classical literati did not write privately for pay, he made a good living selling his literary efforts, including classical funerary inscriptions, poetry and poetry criticism, ghost stories, the cookery book, and even several textbooks of model examination essays that were extraordinary commercial successes.

Once or twice he published or commented on the works of banned poets, a dangerous undertaking in the days of the inquisitions. Over and over again he published and publicly admired the works of women poets, acts that drew irate criticism from contemporary conservative circles.

As Arthur Waley points out, "The one aspect (apart from his genius as a writer) in which Yuan Mei seems to have been unique was his persistence, despite the advice of friends, in publishing writings of a sort that other authors suppressed. It was thought clownish and undignified to print humorous poems, and improper to print references to concubines, young actors, and so on. But in Yuan Mei's view it is the highest duty of a poet to preserve the truth (ts'un ch'i chen) to show all things, himself included, as they really are." Few of Yuan's erotic poems appear in this selection for the simple reason that what is clearly "true" in them is presented in the original through the use of traditional euphemistic language that simply defies translation. The poet's humor and his positions on the natural rights of women, on the dignity of all human life, and on social justice are more abundantly present, if also sometimes veiled. And while some scholars have labeled Yuan Mei as anti-Buddhist, the poems in this collection refute any such interpretation: that Yuan Mei opposed superstition and idolatry is made manifestly clear in "Motto," page 74, a line from which provides the title for this book. That he respected the practitioners of at least one variety of Buddhism is suggested in the same poem. In "The Ancient Bell" and "Late Gazing," among others, he also expresses both a great respect for the tradition of Buddhist practice and what appears to be a call for a rebirth of that practice. That he despised self-promotion and hypocrisy, from behind whatever philosophical or religious façade, is made explicit in poems too numerous to mention.

The particular Buddhist sect that drew his praise, and attracted his own practice, was, not at all surprisingly, the sect called Ch'an in Chinese, more widely known in the contemporary world as Zen. The founder of the school of Confucianism that attracted Yuan Mei, Wang Yang-ming, was accused by the orthodox Neo-Confucians of his own time, as well as those of Yuan's, of being a crypto-Ch'anist. It is an accusation that need not be refuted. Ch'an itself is syncretic, a sort of Taoist Buddhism or Buddhist Taoism, the most "Chinese" of all the East Asian varieties of Buddhism. It is practical, democratic, humorous, and perhaps most importantly of all, open to and even inviting the practice by laymen. The Wei-ma mentioned in several of the specifically "Zen" poems presented here is the Chinese transliteration of Vimalakirti, the famous Indian lay Buddhist, a favorite of Ch'an Buddhists for his very Taoist-like refusal to participate in rarefied philosophical debate. Yuan Mei finds Wei-ma's truth in the thunderous wordlessness of the waterfall on T'ien-t'ai Mountain; he finds it as well in the silently welling pool of human creativity, the acknowledged source of his own poems. There he also finds the Buddha present.

The three ways are here, and they are One. Yuan Mei's poems resolve the paradox. They find beauty and truth in the smallest, and in the greatest, of nature's phenomena. They find spontaneous enjoyment in the small delights and the little challenges offered every human by every day. They demonstrate an ability to find *moral meaning* in *mere phenomena* that denies convincingly the necessity of a supernatural sanction for human existence. This ability arises precisely at the intersection of the practical social commitment and ethical concern of the Confucian with the disciplined attention and humane spirit of the practitioner of Zen.

The poems offered here in translation are the artifacts of a life given form by the Three Ways made One. It was a life lived to the fullest, and observed and reproduced in witty and graceful poems meant to be shared widely. As Waley says, it is a poetry "that even at its lightest always has an undertone of deep feeling and at its saddest may at any moment light a sudden spark of fun."

As a translator of many years' practice, I am humbly aware of the difficulty of translating even apparently simple phrases from the classical Chinese. Strangely, like cultivated euphemisms for sexual practices, conscious wit and humorous irony may also present nearly impossible problems for the translator. I have labored for upwards of ten years on these little poems, and have winnowed more than four hundred "final versions" in English for the roughly one hundred poems presented here. I have tried to emulate Yuan Mei in spirit, to ts'un ch'i chen, and in the process I have found a great deal of real spiritual satisfaction, and some rue. I can only pray that some of the original deep feeling, and some of the fun, will come through to you.

I Don't Bow to Buddhas

Returned from Yang-chou, Up the Hill to View the Snow

I.

There and back, ten days…
The boat returned, with the sun and the river.
Now, to view the snow, I'll go on up the mountain.
Lusting still for idleness, I won't go in the city.

Snow petals brighten the moon's dark face.
Freezing rain sings the Spring's song.
Overnight beside wild rapids
To sound the watches, a single swan.

II.

If you don't climb a thousand crags,
how can you learn
all things are empty?

The mountain's head is white and mine is too.
December dies, the year
runs out its string as all things do.

At the summit: one rude hut, the snow,
this lonely body, and the wind.
I lean on the rail, heart sudden struck:
the moon rises from within Great River: there.

In a Boat: Fearsome Weather

All day in the boat, eyes weary, wide.
Snow petals fall lightly to rest
on floating water weed.
I shut the east window, then peek out on the west,
glad, at least, the wind can't blow
two ways at once.

Idleness

Skinny legs, white plumage, the old egret,
flown before me, in among plum-blossomed boughs.
Great river, floating sky, moon's white connections.
The little boat tied to a tree, breeze in silken strands.
Where there are mountains, I gaze from my window;
when there's no rain, I mount and ride my horse.
Country travel ten full days: I've had a taste of freedom.
Petty official, school teacher, no more,
stealing time, to chant these lines.

Sleepless

Can't get clear of this dream,
can't get sober.

Spring breeze chilly
on the flesh: me all alone.

My orphan sail
finds the bank
where reed flowers fall.

All night
the river sounds
the rain falling:
listen.

After the Bath

After the bath, I lean on the rail.
High clouds hide evening sun.
Somewhere, unseen, it's raining.
Here, just a touch of the cool.

Reading

When I shut a book,
I can be at ease.
If I open one, I agonize.
Books are long, and days are short,
feeling like an ant
who wants to move a mountain,
or a man who waits for dawn-light
with a candle in his hand.

Of ten I read, I might remember one.
The more's the pain,
that in a thousand years
there'll be more books, no end.

So if I wish I were a spirit-being,
or pray Heaven for a few more years...
It's not that I want to dine on dew,
or wander fairy-lands...
Every word that's written:
to read each one: that's all.

At Random in My Garden

Blossoms bring the Spring.
Spring doesn't take them with it
when it goes.

Clouds flow upon the stream.
The stream cannot hold them.

I'd ask why that is,
but no one's here, but
this tall tree,
beneath which I will idle
ponder:
the place:
the Spring:
clouds
go.

Cold Night

Cold night, reading,
forgetting sleep.
The embroidered coverlet has lost its fragrance,
and the brazier's cold.

My lady swallows her anger, but
snatches the lamp away
and asks me,
       "Do you know *what time* it is?"

Monk's Place

At the monk's place
   I lean on
the painted rail.

Eyes roam
    gazing
on the plain.

A little rain
    beyond
a thousand miles.

An evening sun
     reddens
half the village.

Breeze cool,
   a sense of flowers
gathering.

The hall is small,
     the Buddha's
incense mild.

There where last night
     we played
at chess…

On the mossy step
        a fallen man
lies still.

Late Gazing, Looking for an Omen
as the Sun Goes

I.

The window's dark. Roll back the curtain's waves.
What's to be done about sunsets?
Climb up and stand in some high place,
lusting for a little more twilight.

II.

From a thousand houses' cooking fumes,
the Changes weave a single roll of silk.
Whose house, fire still unlit, so late?
Old crow knows whose, and why.

III.

Golden tiles crowd, row on row:
men call this place the Filial Tombs.
Across that vastness, eyes wander:
grand pagoda: one wind-flickering flame.

Lesson

I read a book and learned
to nap by noon, pillowed on
crossed arms. I forgot
to close the window. Silly
me, a heap of fallen flowers.

On a Painting of a White-Haired Old Man

Who'd paint a white-haired ancient?
I smile. I'd rather be a duck.
If you're born with your head snow-white already,
no one can laugh and shout, "You're getting old!"

Spring Day

Blossoms' shade
our shelter deep
entire tower clouds.

Wine for this Memorial Day
and all my guests well drunk.

If you'll not drink
I can only
point you up the mountain:

there
to urge you take your ease today
there is one lonely grave.

So Be It

Blossoms of apricot will perish,
sound of the rain grow quiet.

Moss in the footprints on the path,
its green reflected on my gown.

Wind's fierce,
can't keep the little window shut...

Fallen flowers, pages of poems
together fly away.

I Saw It: I Wrote It

Getting or losing: how to tell which is which?
I lean here smiling softly to the breeze.
The spider so pleased with his artful web
has netted only fallen petals,
not a single bug to eat.

Visiting

Night visit in the mountains,
misty moonlight frozen.
I knock, and before they can answer,
the voice of the Spirit-crane responds.

Writing What I've Seen

All things that live
must make a living.
There's nothing got
without some getting.

From fabled beast to feeble bug
each schemes to make its way.
The Buddha, or the Taoist Sage?
Unending in his labor;

and morning's herald, the rooster, too
can he not cock-a-doodle-do?
I hunger, so I plot to eat;
I'm cold, and would be robed…

But great grand schemes will get you grief.
Take what you need, that's all.
A light craft takes the wind
and skims the water lightly.

A Guest Arrives

A peck, a rap, the rude gate sounds:
I call the boy to sweep the leaves in welcome.
The cold cicada knows the good host's Way:
of Autumn sadness utters not a single cry.

Rolling up the Curtain

I raise curtain on the north window.
The wind blows. Spring's colors are cold.
One monk, one sprig of cloud,
together at Green Mountain's peak.

Sleepless

One, then two, the cocks
              begin to crow.
Fourth watch, fifth watch
              sky not yet lit.
The window just now catching dew,
              east sky turning white.

A sick man's dreams are short
              as winter nights are long.
The lamp snuff lies on the table.
              Mice scuffle on the beams.
Head bowed to pillow,
              my eyes are open wide.
Forty years' worth of things to forget…

Cool Hall

Beating the heat is like hiding from guests:
just stay in the shade in the Hall, and keep quiet.

A few tall Wu-t'ung trees will ward off the sun.
A winding stream will beckon the breeze.

And if, in the heat, guests appear after all...
They might just like to hide here too.

Standing at Night
at the Bottom of the Steps (out of office)

Half bright, half dark, the stars:
> three drops, two drops, the rain.

The Wu-t'ung knows Autumn's come:
> leaf and leaf together whisper.

One page

One page of a book and I'm caught, staying up.
My wife suggests, several times, "Enough is enough."
Ivory tower suffering; my lady's perturbed.
I've grown old. And still just a schoolboy.

Planting Pines

These hands have planted green pines,
> two rows, or three.

I hear it's hard to grow them here,
> beyond Kiangsi.

I'll have to wait to watch
> them burgeoning glory...

But will there be a me
> to see them then?

I cannot see them now
> without that question.

Propped on a Pillow

Propped on a pillow, distant,
in the tatters of a midday dream,
the door is open, yet seclusion's mine.
The guest dismounts with idle play in mind.
Can't he see that I'm already reading?

Climbing the Mountain

I burned incense, swept the earth, and waited
                    for a poem to come...

Then I laughed, and climbed the mountain,
                    leaning on my staff.

How I'd love to be a master
                    of the blue sky's art:

see how many sprigs of snow-white cloud
                    he's brushed in so far today.

Idle Stroll

I break bamboo to make a walking stick,
and wander past the little arbor.
No one around, I talk to myself.
On the stream, a single gull
listens.

Sitting Idle

It rained, and no guest came.
In the empty hall, a single butterfly.

Sitting alone's such a bore:
I've counted every single leaf of Spring.

Alone

The water clock drips the third watch,
                          time runs out.

Frost flowers on the whole broad earth,
                          wind and the trees shiver.

Ancient owl peers in at the door,
                          then chuckles dryly as he leaves.

And here, within, a single lamp, and
                          one old man, sitting.

Rhymes in a Boat

I.

Yesterday the errant wind blew hard against the prow.
The boatmen hauled the tow rope, as cowherd a balky cow.
Today, a lovely breeze, steady from the tail.
We'll make at least a thousand miles, full belly in the sail.
Yesterday I wasn't evil, today no saintly leaven.
In this boat there's only me: I smile upon broad heaven.

II.

From the neighbor's east, an owl's weird cry...
His heart is hard. If he held a spear, the owl would die.
From the neighbor's west, a fox has come
            to yap outside his room.
His heart is set. If he held a bow,
            the fox would meet his doom.
The old monk's meditation ends, by saddest sighs it's marred.
Evil? Not to see it's *easy*: not to hear it's *hard*.

III.

A good horse goes by day, and rests at night.
The sound of oars goes on and on, no end in sight.
When I'm home I flee from guests,
            my gate is always closed.

In a boat I'm home to all,
        to visit, none's disposed.
Thirty-six thousand days
            in the life of a lucky man,
      but a single day that's spent in a boat
      has simply an endless span.

NOTE: *Yuan Mei uses the "heroic couplet" here. It is a very unusual form in Chinese poetry, where the paucity of syllable forms has made rhyming almost too easy. I was amazed to find the poems falling into a regular rhyme pattern in English. I think the doggerel quality is close to what Yuan Mei was shooting for: a formal means of showing his piqued ennui.*

A Bitter Charge

A bitter charge, the old gateman's.
This humble gate is seldom opened wide.
Sometimes though, even he can't stop them.
A whole flock of terns just dropped in.

Just Done

All the heart needs is a home
in which to dwell in quiet.
The flavor of desirelessness
lasts longest.

So a boy runs off
to snatch at floating willow silks...
If he didn't capture them
how could he let them go?

Moss

Daylight never comes here,
yet Spring's arrived:
moss flowers, small as grains of rice,
practice being peonies.

Sleepless

One rain, and all the flowers gone.
Third watch, and all the music still,
except what strikes my ear and stays my sleep:
from a windy branch
the last drops fall.

Autumn Thoughts

Falling sun on empty mountains,
where'd it be good to go?
Monkeys offer creeper, maybe
it's a sign.
Life long wordless, that was
Wei-ma's Way, but I
won't speak of that...

It's just in search of yellow asters
that I've come to see this monk.

Sadness

White-haired, silent; wordless
spring green grave mounds
flag the heart; head bows.
Sadness comes as if it knew the way
quite well, from west of the sunset.

Painting

Here and there I've planted orchids.
Every morning I enjoy my peonies.
And when even these are not enough,
I can paint one more blossom to gaze on.

Sitting at Night

Sitting at night by the west window,
                    rain everywhere.

Before my eyes the rule of nature's bitter,
                    hard to fathom.

The lamp's gentle gleam becomes a pyre:
from all about, moths come,
                    flight upon flight,
                          into the fire.

Passing the Grave of a Friend

Outside the city for Memorial Day rites,
whip dangling, I ride slow along the dike.
Old friends, the so-white snow,
come to earth, without a sound.

Willow Flowers

Willow flowers, snowflakes, the same...
They're feckless.

No matter whose garden they fall in,
They'll always follow the wind away.

Bell

Ancient temple, monks all gone,
the Buddha's image fallen.

The single bell
hangs high in evening's glare.

Sad, so
       full of music…
Ah, just one little tap!
But no one dares.

Egret

The egret stands on the fishing jetty,
alone attends his fancy feather robe.

Slow, steps forward, tries...
Can he really, really fly?

Dog Days

Empty mountain dog day, door shut tight.
Gauze gown, and still I drip with sweat.

Yet I bless the burning wind:
it shrivels visitors.

Long as there's sun, at least
I'll get some writing done.

Night Thought

Midnight, sudden jerk
awake.
Wordless. Heart still, sighs.

Tonight the frost's first fall,
that's all, and I
forgot to cover the houseplants.

Ancient Wall

Ancient Wall at the corner of the courtyard:
passing the years in the shade of the trees,

deep in the dark where no man has seen it,
on the green moss, the smallest of flowers.

Saying Goodbye to a Friend

Years and years, you've come through here
in some hurry. Today, as you mounted to leave
you paused to look at me again.

To let our hands drop from the parting clasp was hard.
Falling tears came easy. Each of us
can count six tens of years.

Sixty

Each year as the year day's passed
I've cocked my ear to hear
the fireworks pop, so sharp, so clear,
all through the night 'til dawn.

This year I didn't listen,
fearing the cock crow's news:
my sixtieth year.

The noise has died now,
to the sound of a page of the calendar turning.
A little time's left. Maybe, just a scrap?

The cock, at least, shows sympathy,
so slow to crow for me.
That's fine. I'll just go on
being fifty-nine.

Rise and Fall

Mountain colors, cold blue leaves,
cold water, leaves fall,
the sun also goes.

The rule of rise and fall is shared
by all save these:

Willow flowers wound and
bound in spider's web, they lie.
No wonder Spring wind
can't make them rise and fall.

Reading

To read a book,
to gaze on flowers,
the two are treasures
I'll be slow to put aside.

The best's to pick a flower
and to vase it on the desk,
to sense the fragrance
while I chant a poem.

Wandering Late at Kulin Temple
(where there was a pleasure house nearby)

The single sound of the bell
brings out the whole hall's monks.

Golden glint of the Buddha's face
almost the flash of a lamp.

The Bodhisattva Dragon Tree is silent,
the wind has died away...

The robes of the monks cast shadows,
as the moon begins to rise.

No need to chant the Sutras
to make the flowers giggle...

As I lean and listen carefully
even the stones respond.

How can the Buddha, King of Emptiness,
boast of setting the whole world free?

Here, when Spring comes,
he hasn't freed even half this pond
from thinking long on love.

On a Painting of the Yellow Millet Dream: A Dream of Wealth and Power

Come causeless, without reason, dreams
are hard to fathom.
Each heart's its own dreams, no two the same.
Had it been I who dreamed there at Hantan,
it wouldn't have been a dream of "wealth" or "power."
I'd have dreamed a book, amidst ten thousand flowers.

Just Done

Done chanting poems,
I paint bamboo.
Tea vapors waft
in the window.

Light clouds may hold
                    a heavy rain.
A single butterfly may explore
                    a pair of flowers.

Just Done

Peaceful body firm afloat
beyond this
floating world.

To go or to stay?
My play
is grave and slow.

The white egret greets my guests for me.
Spring wind rolls up my scroll.

Just Done

A month alone behind closed doors,
forgotten books, remembered, clear again.
Poems come, like water to the pool.
welling, up and out,
from perfect silence.

A Moment

White hair, facing flowers, falling
silent, an anxious heart finds no peace here.
No way to know if next year's blooms
will have this old fool to look after them.
I take the broom in hand to sweep,
and then I stay it, turn
away, but linger by the curving rail…

Full of feeling, birds and butterflies
bear it with me: this Spring chill.

Temple of the Bamboo Grove

Late, I passed the Temple of the Bamboo Grove
In slanting sun the corners of the walls

                                    sunk deep in shade.

Windy lamp, the red unsteady.
Green misty willows, deep and still.
Few monks. Stone chimes are often silent.
Many trees, sunlight and shade too.
Ears catch a hint of Buddhist chanting:
My horse's bells have a pure clear tone.

Conscious of Withering

"Oh, verily, I wither," said Confucius of himself,
and even a thousand of his words
aren't worth one picture of me.
Teeth falling out, the hair at my temples
like feathers molting.
I drag my staff among the flowers,
squint right beneath the lamp at normal print,
inclined to forget what I know I ought to note,
grown accustomed to blithering on and on, and on.
"Ah, how it passes, it passes away," the stream
of life, I heard the Master say.

> And of the saying, "the older the better"?
> Now that's a stupid one.

Twelfth Moon, Fifteenth Night

Be done, be done, the watch
                    drum urges.
Slow, so slowly, sounds
                    of man are gone.
Blow out the light, watch
                    the window brighten.
The moon shines, the whole sky
                    snow.

Given to the Monk Ts'an-ch'un
at Yung-fu Shrine

The coiffure called "the mountain" fills your window.
Here, for hairpin, pines; look there, a light sleeve falls.

Old monk, though you dwell in solitude,
when you come home, there's a Beauty to greet you.

Remembering

The years, their months
turn, grave and slow, their
Fall and Spring, again.

Mountain flowers, mountain leaves and
each time's new.

Sometimes I sit alone,
and smile upon the child I was,

in memory now distant
and a friend.

Delirium (joking at illness)

I don't want to come, yet suddenly I'm here;
I don't want to leave, yet suddenly I'm gone.
Don't know where I've come from, or gone from, either.
In this there is, of course, *True News*.

Since Heaven can't speak, I'll have to pass it on.
Just wait for old Master Chaos to come back to life.
If I search for myself, I'll certainly find me.

Waning Years: Random Poem

Ice on the water,
                windy light,
a fairy-garden Spring.

Memories come one after one.
It's my soul, not the ice,
that's melting.

Youth, pretty child, where did that actor
come from? The one who played
this life of mine straight through?

Waning Years: Random Song

Robes long or short: hat brims wide or narrow.
For thirty years they've grown or shrunk
well beyond all reason.
Now what luck, I've kept these cloaks so long
old fashioned's fashionable again.
These ancient things are all brand new this season.

Late, Walking Alone to a Temple
in the Mountain's Cleft

Green peaks wind around
                    to make a wall.
Though the eaves are dripping from the rain,
                    in the hall there's sunlight.

I look hard, but can't make out
                    the way I came.
I turn, and ask the monk
                    how he got here to greet me.

Laughing at Myself for Lazing Around at West Lake (having started the year with poems planning to go to T'ien-t'ai Mountain with Liu Chih-ping)

It takes a lot of bamboo strips to make a little sail.
It only took a few to make these sandals.
But to get from sailing on West Lake
to climbing up T'ien-t'ai Mountain...

You could say that in my thousand-mile trek to find a Zen Master
I stopped off first down in the country
for a gab with some good old friends.

Ginseng

I love a good logical chat about ethics,
but I won't sit still for a sermon.

Purple Mountain Ginseng's best:
it works, and it doesn't taste so bad.

Near Hao-pa (I saw in the mist a little village of a few tiled roofs, and joyfully admired it)

There's a stream, and there's bamboo,
there's mulberry, and hemp.
Mist-hid, clouded hamlet,
a mild, a tranquil place.
Just a few tilled acres.
Just a few tiled roofs.

How many lives would I
have to live, to get
that simple?

On the Road to T'ien-t'ai

Wrapped, surrounded by ten thousand mountains.
Cut off, no place to go…
Until you're here, there's no way to get here.
Once you're here, there's no way to go.

Gone Again to Gaze on the Cascade

A whole life without speaking,
                    "a thunderous silence"
that was Wei-ma's way.

And here is a place where no monk can preach.

I understand now what T'ao Ch'ien, enlightened,
said he couldn't say.

It's so clear, *here, this water,*
                    my teacher.

Motto

When I meet a monk,
          I bow politely.
When I see a Buddha,
          I don't.

If I bow to a Buddha,
          the Buddha won't know.
But I honor a monk:
          he's here now, apparently,
          or, at least, he seems to be.

Old, and Still Traveling

Old, and still traveling,
                 I'm afraid
I'll forget what I see.

So I make
           these little poems
as travel notes, day after day.

The creeks are so clear:
                 the stones, the sand
could each, could all, be counted.

Rain done,
           the grove's blossoms
send fragrance from their darkness.

The boy is gone.
           Birds perch in
the ox-back shade.

Cart stopped:
           folks sit
the cool beneath the trees.

It worries me and
           I would ask,
whose burial mounds are these?

Stone men there
    are speechless,
napping in the evening sun.

Cloud Creek

Clouds come
     play with mountain peaks,
and peak and peak
     that were at war
become, at Change's wont,
     a flowing stream
no sandals such as mine
     can cross.

You Have to Pass "Forty-nine Turns to the Top" Peak Before You Get to Wild Goose Mountain

Forty-nine turns to the peak
wind and coil up toward heaven.

If you begrudge your feet some pain
you'll miss ten thousand peaks.

Now, where I tread there is no earth:
the only summit, the torrent.

Three stops before you reach the top.
Hat and robe soaked through:

the clouds and mist.

Jade Lady Peak

Wind combed, cloud wrapped,
dressed wet
        with rain,
a casual do
        by the moonlight.

But don't say Jade Lady
        will never grow old:
this Autumn she's frost
at her temples.

At the Narrows of the Yung-chia River

For three miles folks' houses
practically straddle the river,
scattered among stones and blossoms,
the householders' hedges.

Their low bramble gates are a little like
the rich man's crimson portals:
you'll have to bow and scrape a bit
if you ever want to enter.

Mountain Travel: Random Song

Ten miles of rugged road, steep hills
for every mile of flat.

One crag sees me off as
one crag greets me.

Green mountains' tight cocoon
to bind me.

I can't believe that up ahead
there's any road to go.

Mountain Wandering

Sunlit, mountains stand straight up.
Mountains sink in rain.
Rising, I like sunlight best;
for roaming, give me shade.

Here's the sort of pale blue,
deep green place Wang Wei might paint:
there's no *way* to sing it.

A Quatrain in Six-Character Lines

Face powder's not as white as snow.
Incense will never rival flowers' fragrance.
Man's world and heaven are not the same.
It's not worth six more words.

NOTE: Five- and seven-syllable lines are the standard. Six is uncommon.

83

At "Be Careful" Bank

The dangerous bank is
                hard to get over…
Careful indeed,
        we help each other up.

Might we, on flat ground, too,
go on as we do when we're here?

By Accident

I've seen every temple here,
asked nothing, as the Buddha knows.

But the moon came
            as if to rendezvous,
and the clouds went off
            without goodbyes.

In the inns a decent bite to eat
was hard to come by,
but in my carriage
poems came freely.

Going back, the baggage will be heavier:
two or three seedlings of pine.

Talking Art

In painting it's catching the "spirit" and "essence."
In poems that's "nature" and "feelings."

An elegant dragon, with its life's breath gone?
Better a rat, with some scurry left in him.

On Trading My Poems for Autumn Orchids

I promised to trade poems
for southern posies.
The two seemed
clearly equal pledges.
The trade was made
and then I felt regrets.

The blossom of the brush
will waft perfume
far beyond the Fall.

The Peak of Lonely Elegance

Dragon veins, the mountain ranges:
here, just the dragon, the vein run out.
And suddenly the single peak, poking southern stars.

At Kueilin the mountain shapes, all crazy
spikes and knobs. The Peak of Lonely Elegance
is one to cap them all.

Three hundred and six steps to mount it,
the one town down below,
with hearth-fire smoke to greet the eye.

The green mountain stands there,
taut as a tuned lute string.

In one's own life, to stand so straight,
so lonely... What harm, though, to try?

P'u-t'o Temple

A temple, hidden, treasured

                    in the mountain's cleft.

Pines, bamboo,

             such a subtle flavor:

the ancient Buddha sits there, wordless.

The welling springs speak for him.

Day After Day

Day after day strange peaks
greet me, passing.
I can't paint, can only sing them here.

But can an old man bear,
after gazing on the mountains,
to find his heart so full of stones?

Whose House

In someone's house
          the quiet singing,
jade chimes tinkling, crystal screen.

The lilting pipes,
          the pure, clear strings,
all night long, no stopping.

But the song will end
          as men's lives do.
How to bear it? The white-
          haired traveler listens.

They Mock Me for Planting Trees at My Age

Seventy, and still planting trees...
Don't laugh at me, my friends.
Of course I know I'm going to die.
I also know I'm not dead yet.

Going Down from Fort Tu-hsia to Hen Cave I Gazed Back at the Towers and Pavilions and Felt Like I Was Floating in the Sky

Mist masked vague towers still
there, but lost in that vastness.
To go back would be hard.
That's life…
         Come down from
high places, you'd better
not look back.

Rain Passes

Rain passes, washing the face of the mountain.
Clouds come, the mountain's in a dream.
Clouds and rain come and go as they please.
Only the mountain, forever green, remains.

Leaning on the Railing

All day leaning,
        smiling,
looking out.

This world's every
            thing's
too hard to tell.

Stones in the stream
can't be countless.

Surely some
spirit could count them.

Quatrain

For formal occasions, "I'm too old."
For an impromptu picnic, young enough.

They say you're as old as you act...
But I can't keep my friends from smirking.

Something to Ridicule

Mencius tells us that Confucius, too,
like all the other men of Lu, fought for his share
of what was taken in the hunt: it was
the custom there. To keep oneself in cloisters just
to seek a name for uprightness...that
lacks a certain dignity.

But getting learning, too, may be
but putting make-up on.
If one's a whore at heart, he's
sure to act the part.

Falling Leaves

These Autumn leaves are like old men:
huddled, doting on the dregs of day.

One frost, and they'll all come falling.
Some will come soon, the others later.

Mornings Arise

Mornings, I rise
to find ten thousand kinds
of pleasures.

Evenings sleep: the single
mantra – now, the heart is
nothingness.

No knowing in this world
which of these ten thousand things
is me.

On a Painting

Rush hut,
bamboo grove,
field song,
all four sides.

Peach Blossom Spring's the
Paradise, within:
so why so few who
find the way?

Answering

The wine we spilled before the lamp last night
is not yet dry.
Now the dew of dawn lies damp
on the traveler's saddle.
You turned back to ask some little question.
I am old. It was hard to answer.

Speaking My Mind

I.

When the clouds come the mountain
        "ontologically dismanifests."
When they go (I guess) it exhibits its
        phenomenological "mountainness."
Do you suppose
        the mountain knows?

II.

Oh perhaps the fabled P'an Ku made the world,
but before the Farmer Spirit had tilled one field,
bored to death with the time on his hands,
the Great Fu Hsi brushed the single stroke
of the first written word. He's the one
who really got things going.

III.

To learn to be without desire
        you must desire that.
Better to do as you please:
        sing idleness.
Floating clouds, and water running...
        Where's their source?
In all the vastness of the sea and sky,
        you'll never find it.

Old, and Traveling

At my age to go ten thousand miles
I will admit takes gall.
Singing toward a thousand peaks,
I sometimes shy away.

But I would add that notable peaks
share this with noteworthy men...
only a fool, having met with one,
will not find it hard to part.

Sick (November eighteenth)

One little bout of illness
won't carry me off, but I *am* old,
and I'm not surprised the family is a trifle nervous.
Half a dozen quacks called in,
the kids attending me through half the night.

But the oldest tree knows all about the wind and frost,
and an idle cloud knows best of comings and goings.
This cold cicada's still got both his shrilling wings:
see how his song still sounds the same?

Sick (I find I can't stand to read anything but my own collected works)

Sick, what could be more
fitting than to read?
I have just enough strength left
to open a book.

My ear is pleased to catch
the sound of birds outside the window.
My heart rejoices to be reading
my own poems.

One life's signs and traces,
here, and here again.
Ten thousand miles of wandering footprints,
leading everywhere.

The chanting done, six thousand and
three hundred poems!
Heart ablaze with dreams of Spring,
I've traveled back in time.

Bothered by My Dreams, I Wrote This in Six-Word Lines

Awake I get damned few ideas.
In dreams I find great lines,
but as I slowly come awake,
they sink right out of sight.

Just like chasing a dead man.
What's gone is, face it, gone.

Fifteenth Night of the Second Moon

A fragrance in the darkness, east,
scattered shadows by the curving rail.

A thousand trees of flowering plum,
and one old man,

white hair like blossoms,
blossoms like a heavy snow.

Late at night, it's hard to know what's what
in the brightness of the moon.

Furs in the Sixth Month

Spreading lotus leaves
float full the pond.
The season moves into midsummer,
but I feel the chill of Fall.

Fate decrees an old man
should look like one. This year
July arrives, and
I'm still wrapped in fur.

Last Poem: Goodbye to My Garden

Was I no more than some fairy-being,
strange beast from the *Sutra of Ceylon*,
arisen and set free to play
in Hsiao-ts'ang's summit garden?

Did I not know that garden's guests
of poems and lutes, wine and songs
would also hear the gong of time,
the last dripped drop of the water clock?

My eye roams the towers and pavilions,
and I know these lines are my farewell.
This mountain full of birds will stay,
forever wound and bound in its flowers.

Long ago an Immortal chose to return
to his home in the form of a crane,
and was almost shot down by a lad with a sling.
If I ever come back to this Paradise,
I'll remember to be careful.

ABOUT THE TRANSLATOR

Born in Lafayette, Indiana, in 1941, J.P. Seaton has taught Chinese at the University of North Carolina, Chapel Hill, since 1968. Among his several volumes of translations are *Love & Time: Poems of Ou-yang Hsiu* (Copper Canyon Press, 1989), *Chinese Poetic Writing*, *The View from Cold Mountain*, and *The Wine of Endless Life*. He is co-editor of *A Drifting Boat: Chinese Zen Poetry*, and a contributor to numerous anthologies and journals. He lives in the woods, in a little house off of Chicken Bridge Road in Pittsboro, North Carolina, where conversation, poetry, wine and music are sampled in the ancient tradition.

BOOK DESIGN and composition by John D. Berry and Jennifer Van West, using Adobe PageMaker 6.0, a Power Computing Power 120, and a Macintosh IIVX. The type is Quadraat, an original digital typeface designed by Fred Smeijers and released in 1992 by FontShop International as part of their FontFont library. Quadraat displays the subtle irregularities of a handmade face, which make it particularly readable at small sizes and give it a distinctive character at large sizes.